Forgo

The Cherelle Clarke Story

First Edition Design Publishing

Forgot to Say Goodbye
Copyright ©2014 Lisa Seymour

ISBN 978-1622-875-37-5 PRINT
ISBN 978-1622-875-38-2 EBOOK

LCCN 2014933238

February 2014

Published and Distributed by
First Edition Design Publishing, Inc.
P.O. Box 20217, Sarasota, FL 34276-3217
www.firsteditiondesignpublishing.com

Edited by Marci Messick

ALL RIGHTS RESERVED. No part of this book publication may be reproduced, stored in a retrieval system, or transmitted in any form or by any means — electronic, mechanical, photo-copy, recording, or any other — except brief quotation in reviews, without the prior permission of the author or publisher.

Cherelle Clarke

November. 25, 1994 to April 2, 2009

Forgot to Say Goodbye

The Cherelle Clarke Story

By Lisa Seymour

CHAPTER 1
The Birth of an Angel

Do you ever wonder why children are taken back to Heaven at such young ages? I ask myself why every day and never get an answer. My name is Lisa Seymour and this is the story of my oldest daughter who committed suicide at the age of fourteen on April 02, 2009 and the tragic events that led up to her death.

I had three beautiful children, all out of wedlock: two girls and one boy. I loved them all unconditionally and didn't regret having any one of them. I'd give my life for any of them.

Cherelle and Cheyenne shared the same biological father, DeVaughn, Dee for short. The girls were 1 year and 8 days apart, but their sizes were a world apart. Cherelle took after her father, 5 feet, 4 inches tall, and 125 pounds. Cheyenne, on the other hand, is more petite.

The girls' father, Dee, presents himself as a tough black man standing 6 feet 2 inches tall and weighing over 200 pounds. He was about 4 years younger than me, but I wasn't too concerned about ages at the time. He was the kind of guy that gave you chills and that could make the hair on the back of your neck stand on end. He was a fascinating man to me, the type of man that I had never dated before, and I wasn't quite sure how my parents would react to him. They didn't know that I had a preference for black men at that time, but they were going to find out sooner than later, when I found myself pregnant with Cherelle.

Darrien, my son, was my youngest. He had a different father than the girls'. His father's name was Joseph Corley. He, too, was a big black man standing 6 feet tall with a dark complexion and a shaven head and dark eyes. I was with Darrien's father for eight years before I lost him to a suicide tragedy on April 03, 2004.

Cherelle's life began on a cold day where the sky was grey and the breeze blew through the leafless trees. It was November 25, 1994, Thanksgiving Day. The pain that I felt like no more than cramping began at 5 a.m., but I was able to ignore them, even though they were coming every ten minutes. There was no way I was going to miss Thanksgiving dinner at my sister's house. I showered and dressed like every other day. I drove to my sister Debi's house in Glenville, New York like usual. I met everyone at my sister's house, including my mother and father. It was our Thanksgiving tradition. The pain became greater throughout the day. I tried to ignore the contractions, but they started to feel like someone was putting a wedge in my gut every so often until they became full out contractions. Yes, I finally admitted contractions; then there was no hiding them. However, I did get to eat my Thanksgiving dinner prior to going to the hospital.

Panic rose throughout the house. Everyone started to yell and run around like kids in a candy shop. Everyone was deciding who was going to bring me to the hospital as I sat there like a dog waiting to be let out. Finally my mother decided or was chosen to bring me to the hospital; maybe she pulled the small straw out of a hat; I don't know, but off to the hospital we went. I was brought to St. Clare's hospital in Schenectady, New York for the birth of my first child. We called my boyfriend, Dee, to meet us there. The ride was horrible and my water even broke in the truck. That was really gross. We arrived approximately twenty minutes later. My mother was in a panic; running into the hospital like her head was cut off. A nurse assisted us; and made me comfortable in a small room, well, as comfortable as one with back labor could be. Man! I never felt so much pain; besides those broken ribs I had a few months back, and I never want them again. Ha ha.

Anyways, Dee finally arrived some time later. I lost track of time; every minute seemed like an hour. I never did attend those birthing classes, but maybe I should have because, Dee thought it would have been cute to try to help me breathe.

"Breathe" he would say.

"Breathe"…

Man, I wanted to strangle him.

The pain was unbearable; I was only dilated 3 centimeters at 8:00 p.m. and again at 1:00 a.m. The Doctor thought that I would have to be induced. At this point I was given medication to help me relax with each labor pain. The contractions became faster, from seven minutes apart to five. The Doctor was called in around 3:15; I was finally 9 centimeters dilated. A baby was on the way. I dilated my last centimeter and pushed three times, and there she was on the table. My eyes were swollen from crying, but at 3:50 a.m. I had a beautiful 8 pound, 7 ounce girl with a full head of dark brown curly hair and brown eyes. She was gorgeous. Her name was Cherelle Allie Clarke. I was now a proud mother. It was all worth it.

The first words I said were "Look at all her hair!" and her father said, "Where are you taking her?" as the Doctors took Cherelle away to be checked out.

Cherelle Allie Clarke: first name chosen by me when I had a dream in October 1994 that I had a child named Cherelle. Allie was chosen by her father after his great grandmother.

Cherelle's developmental milestones were age appropriate, although she seemed busier than the average child. Cherelle sat without support at approximately 4 months of age and began to creep at 6 months. Her first 3 steps were taken on October 17, 1995, and she walked alone on October 24, 1995. Cherelle was potty trained by 18 months and spoke her first words, Dada, Mama, Bye-bye, and her favorite word, hi, at 1 year old. The most precious words Cherelle ever spoke were "I love you" on August 15, 1996. Cherelle's behaviors when she was young, like around the terrible 2 stages were horrendous. She used to have temper tantrums and throw herself backwards flat on the floor and kick. She loved to play with others, but when it came to sharing, hands off, her body language would say. Cherelle was also physical with her friends and family at times by hitting, pulling hair, and of course, pulling Grandma's glasses right off her face when she least expected it. Cherelle also wasn't a great listener when it came to "Don't Touch!" but is any child really that well-behaved all the time?

When Cherelle was young she was fixated with picking up fuzzies off the floor and putting them in her mouth. It was the craziest thing, but she always had to be supervised for this reason. Cherelle was also had obsessed with Barney; she loved that big purple dinosaur. One other thing Cherelle started early in life was her love of books, which eventually brought her good grades in school.

CHAPTER 2
Moving around Town

Our family moved around a lot when Cherelle was alive. The very first house Cherelle lived in was on Torrington Avenue in Rotterdam, New York. This was a two bedroom basement apartment with a bathroom, living room, and a kitchen for Cherelle and me. I only stayed there for approximately one year. I decided I needed to be closer to my mother.

The Burnt Hills community was close to my parent's home, so I decided to search there for housing. I found a two story house on Saratoga Road. It was much too big for just Cherelle and me, but I was pregnant with my second child. I grabbed a job waitressing across the street from this house, and my mother watched Cherelle when I worked. The rent exceeded my income and we had to move again, but not before I had Cheyenne.

I then moved to Alita Drive in Glenville, New York, a nice small, one-family home around the corner from my parents. However, the basement smelled of mold and we had to leave.

I took Cherelle and her sister back to Schenectady. We found a nice place on Eastern Avenue. It was a two bedroom upstairs apartment. Cherelle and her sister shared a year until the Landlord, who lived downstairs, stated that the children were 'too loud over their heads' and asked us to leave.

In September 1996, DeVaughn, the girls' father and I broke up, but we remained friends. The girls still lived with me, but I never held them away from him. We had our differences that we just could not agree upon. So we went our separate ways.

CHAPTER 3
New Step-Father

It was a brisk day in November 1996 when I met this man named Joseph Corley, who became the man I fell in love with, the man of my dreams. He was a tractor trailer driver, driving the big 54-foot trailers.

I at first I didn't like Joe; actually, I really couldn't stand him; he was too pushy. He kept asking for my telephone number and I would not give it to him, but I eventually gave in. We started dating in November 1996 until his death in April 03, 2004.

What made Joe special in my eyes was that he accepted Cherelle, and Cheyenne like they were his own children. He never treated Darrien any differently; they were all his.

Cherelle lost contact with Dee when she was three years old; however, Joe was there to fill in the gaps; Cherelle called Joe "Daddy Joe" and became very close with Joe.

Anyways, off again we went, searching for another place in Schenectady and I found that place resting on a dead end street on Avenue B. It was a nice one-family, two bedroom home. The girls nestled together in bunk bed and I had my own bed. At this point Cherelle was 4 years old. She played all the time with Cheyenne, her older cousin Brianna, and her younger twin cousins, Shauna and Sarah.

Since Joe worked driving out over the road a lot, we didn't see him some of the time. Anyways, we stayed at Avenue B for one year until our son was born in 1998. Then the house became too small. So the search began again.

Joe and our new family moved to Cobleskill, New York in 1999.

Cobleskill was approximately forty minutes from Schenectady. It was a small town made up of 99% Caucasian, but that didn't stop us.

We moved into a huge Victorian, one-family home. Cherelle loved to run up and down the wrap-a-round stair case, down the long hallway to the back staircase that led to the kitchen, through the dining room, into the den, through the living room, out to the hallway, and back up the front stairs again, with her siblings running close behind. Cherelle was still four, but able to enter kindergarten at Ryder Elementary School. She didn't have any problem fitting in. She really enjoyed participating in her half-day at school and was a good student as well. Cherelle received her Kindergarten diploma from Ryder Elementary School.

Cherelle enjoyed having her school friends over to the house, and most of all she loved the swing set we had bought for the kids for the back yard. Cherelle would run full speed around the yard with the warm breeze blowing through her hair. She ran to the swing and belly flopped onto it, face down as if to fly like a bird. At the age of five, Cherelle was 3 feet, 9 inches tall and weighed 50 pounds. Her first pet was a "shit." Well, if you asked Cherelle at that time, she'd say her fish was a "shit" because she couldn't pronounce "fish." It was hilarious. Her second pet was a Hermit crab named "Hi," because she would point and say "hi" to it.

Cobleskill also brought heartache to the family. I bought the children a little black mixed puppy that escaped out the front door and was hit by a car and killed instantly. It was horrifying. So I went out one day to Wal-Mart, and what do you know, there were mixed lab puppies for free. I had to have one. So I took one impulsively and brought it home. The children loved and cuddled him and named him Grizzle. Well, the inevitable happened. He, too, ran out into the road and BANG! He got hit. He too died instantly. I gave up at that point. It wasn't meant to be.

When Cherelle was six years old, my Dream house was ripped away from me. The house was bought from under Joe and me after we thought long and hard on purchasing it. Sooo…

Off again we went looking for another roof to put over our childrens' heads. This time we checked out modular homes. They were very interesting Pre-fab homes and all we had to do was find land to place the house on, but we never found that perfect spot because I was picky and wanted a lot of land for horses, of course. So we stuck with houses.

Joe and I found another place to reside in Cobleskill for a while. We found a small, two-story, house in the heart of Cobleskill on Lark Street. It was nothing like the huge Victorian home we just left, but we made it our home. Unfortunately, the front porch beams were falling down and eventually toppled over on Joe, injuring him. Sooo… we had to leave due to safety concerns.

CHAPTER 4
In Motion Again

In 2001 we ended up moving to the Catskills, for God only knows for what reason. Joe was still working as a tractor trailer driver, so the children and I rented a very small, three-bedroom, one story house, which had a lot of land. This house was located in Leeds-Athens in Catskill, New York, next to the Thruway.

Cherelle was seven years old now and in first grade in Irving Elementary School in the Catskills. She adjusted well, but I got lonely out there all by myself, without Joe's company or even my family's presence. However, Cherelle had made friends with a few children, who frequently visited—she remained a social butterfly.

Days turned into weeks, which turned into months and now it was time to return to good old Schenectady. It was spring time once again, where the flowers fight to come back to life and the birds come out to sing. I had to move back closer to my family. I had missed them so much. I pulled Cherelle out of first grade and we moved back home.

Joe came off the road in 2001 and did local trucking while I started my new job in the field of Occupational Therapy. Cherelle was eight years old when she started attending Van Corlaer Elementary School. She, once again, adjusted quite well. She never seemed to have a problem adjusting to her surroundings or making friends. She was a happy-go-lucky child.

When Cherelle finished first grade, I made the decision to buy my own home, something to call my own. So yes, we moved again, this time to 806 Bradt Street--my first home. It was a large, four-bedroom house with two bathrooms, a living room, kitchen, dining room, large basement and attic. It also had a large yard and garage and ghosts! Yes, I said ghosts, but that's a whole other story book.

All the kids had their own rooms. Cherelle was the oldest child, so she got first pick, chose the largest. She loved to decorate her room. It was decorated with pink and purple throughout, with pink curtains and a matching bed set. Cherelle had a small room off her closet that the girls would use as a play room for their American Girl dolls and baby dolls.

Cherelle entered Martin Luther King Elementary School for second grade only and successfully completed it. She received an award at the end of the year for 100% Spelling Average all year, Best girl math student, Math Facts Wiz, Most Social and a Certificate of Achievement from D.A.R.E. program. She made me so proud.

DeVaughn entered Cherelle's life, once again, in 2003, when she was around eight years old and still living at Bradt Street with Daddy Joe. She didn't quite know how to relate to her father after he was missing for so many years, and as she got older, Cherelle began to rebel against her father. I tried to talk to Cherelle about how important it was to see her father and how he wanted to be a father to her, but she refused quite frequently when he asked her to go out and at times, he would force her to go, making the situation worse. It was heartbreaking to watch because DeVaughn wanted to bond with Cherelle and she wouldn't give him a chance.

When Cherelle was nine years old, I enrolled her in the International Charter School of Schenectady. She had to wear a uniform at this school, but that didn't seem to bother her that much. She made a lot of close friends at this school, and a few went through to High School together. She also had a great best friend, Brianna, out of school; they were inseparable. I lost the house to foreclosure, after my significant other, Joe, committed suicide in 2004.

Cherelle continued to do well in school. She remained on the honor roll every quarter and was above grade level in 3rd grade in Math and English, as well as other grades. In 2003 Cherelle received an Academic Award, Code of Conduct Award, and Achievement in Student Life Award.

CHAPTER 5
Hard Times

Cherelle wasn't handling Joe's death very well. One night she broke a picture frame and took a small piece of glass and started cutting her wrist. I was horrified. Not knowing what to do or where to turn I called my mother. Cherelle seemed to be depressed, but this cutting occurrence seemed to be a one-time thing. However, I did seek the professional help from Northeast Parent and Child Society Child Guidance Center.

I now have in my possession all of the documentation from all of Cherelle's individual counseling sessions from Northeast Parent and Child Society and Child Guidance Center also known as Child Guidance

When Cherelle was eleven years old she presented with an onset of depressive symptoms that started after Joe died in April 2004. She was very close to Joe, she said to her therapist. She said that she was mad at him that morning and she forgot to say goodbye that day and that may be related to why he hanged himself. Cherelle also expressed that she thinks about hanging herself to be with him; however, she doesn't think she would ever do it because of the effect it would have on her family.

Child Guidance placed Cherelle on medication right away, along with weekly individual counseling. My mother and I religiously brought her there, without question.

We noticed great improvements in her overall mood since she started the antidepressants. Her affect was brighter and she was more playful and talkative; however, Cherelle continued to have thoughts of suicide and cutting herself. I don't know why she was never hospitalized!!!

CHAPTER 6
Family Ties Broken

In 2006 I had to make a decision that was heart breaking for me, but might just have saved my daughter's life. I had to get her into new surroundings to get her mind off of Joe and his death. I sent Cherelle to my parent's house. She lived there and I came to see her or she came to see me on the weekends. She was no longer affiliated with Schenectady Schools or her friends; Cherelle went to Burnt Hills Jr. High.

Cherelle was just twelve years old when she started living with my parents in Glenville. It was the same old house I grew up in and she attended Burnt Hills Junior Schools, like I had so many years ago. The only difference was that Cherelle was half black, making life in a mostly white and rich environment more challenging. However, she was successful making some new friends and even performed in the chorus and in the drama club's play "Peter Pan," where she was a pirate. Her grades were remarkable, only missing the President's List by .5; unbelievable. Words couldn't express how proud I was of my daughter. The only problem Cherelle presented with is that she inherited my naivety. I prayed to God to protect her from being a victim, like I was.

While Cherelle was at my mother's house she had written a story. We're not sure if it was for a school project or not, because it was never graded, but let me inform you, it was a really great story for her age and I would like to share it with you…

"I Had a Strange Dream"
By Cherelle Clarke

My mom said that she had to go to a party with my dad so I had to baby sit my brother and sister. By the way, I'm Cherelle and as you can see I have a brother and sister named Darrien and Cheyenne. Back to the story now! I put them to sleep around 8:30 and stayed up and watched TV to about 9:30. Then I fell asleep.

I woke up in a house that wasn't mine; I've never seen it before. I started looking around for my brother and sister; I couldn't find them. I started freaking out. I ran into the bathroom for a drink of water. The people that lived there had a full length mirror on the back of the door. I turned around and saw that I wasn't twelve anymore. I fell down and started screaming. I looked thirty years old.

I walked back into the room I was in when I woke up. A man was in the bed and said "Honey are you okay?" I screamed and ran out of the house. The mailman walked by and gave me some mail. Most of them said Cherelle Clarke, but one of them said Cherelle and James Clarke. I noticed that I lived in that house and that man in that bed was my husband. I walked back into the house.

I said, "Mr. Clarke, I don't know who you are, I don't know where I am, and I don't know what happened. I was twelve years old when I went to bed last night, but when I woke up I'm thirty years old."

"Alright, whatever you say," James said. Then a dog came running down the hallway and jumped up on me. He is so cute; I wish he was mine, I thought to myself.

I asked, "Whose dog is this?"

"It's ours honey, you must of really hit your head hard yesterday!" said James. Then three kids came running down the hallway screaming 'mommy…'

"I'm sorry; I'm not your mom!"

"Your funny!" exclaimed the oldest child. I gave them a look like 'what are you talking about, I'm not joking'.

"The oldest child is Chris; he is ten years old, the middle child is Roxanne, but we call her Roxy, she is eight years old, the youngest child is Laura, she is five years old, and the dog is Rocky, who is an English Bull Mastiff, she is sixteen weeks old," James said sarcastically. I fainted because they were all crowed around me. I woke up and they were all staring at me like I had a mole on my face. I looked at them and I saw a similarity between me and the kids in our own different way. I started to cry and then I hugged them! I helped them get ready for school that morning. Laura and Roxy were the first ones to leave on their bus. I still thought 'Where I am and where are my sister and brother.' I thought if I keep playing along with these crazy people, I can get out of here and find my mom, dad, sister, and brother.

I went into Chris's room; he still wasn't dressed.

"Why aren't you dressed yet, your bus will be here in twenty minutes?" I said anxiously

I don't want to go to school today, mom. I'm too tired and don't feel good at all!" said Chris.

"Well, I don't know why you don't want to go to school, who does, but you have to go; it's very important that you get your education." I said.

"Okay, I'll go just because you talked me into It." said Chris.

"Now hurry up your bus will be here in fifteen minutes!" I exclaimed.

"Yes mom." said Chris.

When he got downstairs he hurried up and ate two pieces of French toast. The bus came; he grabbed his backpack and said good-bye while he got on the bus. James left about ten minutes after Chris left. I started looking around the house for anything strange. The only thing strange was my senior year book, but I don't remember being in my senior year. I found a whole bunch of pictures of me and the crazy people that were here are my family. How strange is that!!

I went to my address where I lived with my mom, dad, sister, and brother. I rang the doorbell. Some women answered the door but she wasn't my mom.

"Mr. and Mrs. Clarke do they still live here, and if they don't can you tell me where they moved?" I asked very eager, but polite.

I'm so sorry sweetheart, the Clarke's and their children, besides one, got in a car accident. They all died about half an hour after the accident. I'm so sorry!" the lady told me. I wouldn't believe it so I ran to the library and checked the newspapers about four years ago. There it was the article about the accident my family was in.

I ran back to my house with tears falling down my cheeks. When I got there the family was in the living room. They asked what was wrong, and I said "Nothing." Then I just hugged them so hard. I told them I loved them.

That night when we all went to bed, I had a great sleep. I woke up to somebody calling my name. I said, "James "Stop it." Then the person who was like James said "Whose James." I woke up and I said "Mom." I went back to my twelve year old self again. My mom, my dad, my sister, and my brother were all crowding around me. Then I hugged them all so tight. I told them that they were all in my dream. I told them all about it. My sister and brother said "What a weird dream." and I said "I know."

Wasn't that a cute story? Anyway, while Cherelle remained at my parent's she was very active in school sports; well at least she tried. She wasn't too graceful.

She participated in field hockey, crew, in which she tipped over the boat, and cheerleading with the Belmont Pop Warner for two years and even went to sectionals.

Cherelle made a lot of friends while she stayed in Burnt Hills Junior High School. One particular girlfriend was Sarah. They became really close friends, but lost contact when Cherelle moved back to Schenectady. It was a shame because good friends are hard to find, and she was a really good influence on Cherelle.

I hated the arrangement of Cherelle living at my parent's house. Cherelle remained there for seventh and eighth grade. She excelled at her school work while she was there, but I felt that our relationship was falling apart. I missed her so much, and at that time I needed my other two children so much that Cherelle felt left out. It wasn't true.

CHAPTER 7
Family on the Move Again

When I lost my home on Bradt Street, Cheyenne, Darrien, and I moved a few blocks away into an upstairs flat that also occupied the attic that was used as a fourth bedroom so that Cherelle had her own room when she would come home to visit.

While we lived on Broadway, I had bought the children a Thoroughbred horse; his name was Danny O'Shay, nick named, "Danny Boy." He was a seven-year-old chestnut thoroughbred, who was abused; he was a big boy compared to my children, standing 16.1. My children just loved him to pieces; however, when I went on disability I no longer could afford him and we had to get rid of him. Man, did I not only disappoint and rip out the heart of my children but of myself as well. It was a very hard time, like we lost a member of our family.

We stayed at Broadway for another year then moved to 212 Victory--into the Ghetto we went. It was a nice three-bedroom apartment, but it was pricey and the landlord complained about EVERYTHING, especially the dog. I couldn't wait to get out.

We lasted for eleven months at 212 Victory, to be exact, and then a great opportunity arose across the street. A three-bedroom flat, with a large front room; which I could turn into my room, was for rent and the landlord was cool. Perfect, just what I needed. I wanted Cherelle home, and that's what we decided to do.

This flat was huge. Starting at the back of the house was the kitchen, which the girls and I painted red and white at one point, and off the kitchen was Darrien's bedroom. On opposite side of the kitchen was the dining room and off the dining room was Cherelle's bedroom. The other side of the dining room led to the living room, and within the living was a large attached room, which I had made my bedroom. Also off the living room was Cheyenne's bedroom and the front door access. I also had access to the basement, where my washer and dryer were located. So as you see, it was a decent size flat, and we lived there for two years until Cherelle passed. Then I believe it was too much for my other children to live in the same house their sibling had killed herself in. I never wanted to move, but I had to for my children's' wellbeing.

Well, my daughter Cherelle came back home to Schenectady to live at 213 Victory with us family once again. She was thirteen years old now.

My parents were very disappointed in Cherelle and me for our decisions, but we really did miss each other and she wanted to go to Schenectady High School for her 9th grade year.

CHAPTER 8
Coming Home

The summer of 2008 was a new experience for Cherelle. She ran amuck like a wild mustang does in the warm summer breeze. Cherelle had a few really close friends then that still come over to my house to this day, such as Hailey, Taylor, Justice, and Tynisha (Tiny for short).

By the time Cherelle moved back home her weight dropped from one hundred and sixty five pounds to a hundred and thirty pounds. When she passed away she weighed one hundred and twenty five, totaling a loss of 45 pounds.

Cherelle met her first steady boyfriend, Duane, over the summer. He was a quite young boy. He was Cherelle's first boyfriend and she just adored him, maybe too much. He became her world. Duane didn't realize what an impact that he had over Cherelle's life. As she had written in her diary, "I can't live without him!" Duane and Cherelle saw each other just about every day without question. She would walk the few blocks to his house and stay all day until her 8:30 curfew. Cherelle just adored this boy.

One night over the summer while I was out with a friend, I received a frantic call late at night. It seemed that my friend, who was watching my children at home, let Cherelle out of the house to walk the Hill to her boyfriend Duane's house. On her way home after midnight, Cherelle was jumped. It turns out that the girls who jumped her had to do it for an initiation into the gang that called themselves 'Hill Bitches', part of the 'The 4-Block Gang'. In turn, Cherelle plead with us and her therapist at Child Guidance not to go to the police because she said it would happen again if she went to the police, and it would be even worse next time. We believed her, even though she received two broken ribs and a slight concussion.

Cherelle was a happy-go-lucky child until she moved back home. Over the summer of 2008 we began to see her whole demeanor change; she had lost a total of over 45 pounds, dressed, walked and communicated differently. She also began to isolate herself from friends and family, and she rarely smiled or laughed like she used to. She just wasn't the 'Relly Belly' we knew.

Cherelle continued individual therapy until November 21, 2006, when Northeast Parent & Child Society changed her status to 'medication only' until January 09, 2009. That's when I made an appointment with them, as Cherelle had cut the words "FAT, UGLY, STUPID" onto her stomach with a piece of glass. By all means, she wasn't any of these.

Cherelle wasn't happy anymore at all. Finding her diary after her death, I realized how unhappy she really was. If only I read her diary I might have saved her life by putting her in the hospital. I'll never know, but I do know that Cherelle had attempted to hang herself three other times before she succeeded on the fourth try.

In the beginning of February 2009 the family bunny died, and Cherelle took it hard. She ran to her room and closed the door; I didn't think anything of it. Later that day Cherelle came out of her room with "RIP" cut into her wrist. I was horrified. "Why did you do that?" I asked. Cherelle stated, "I was sad."

From that day on Cherelle continued to cut her wrists, stomach and forearms to release her feelings of sadness and anger. In therapy she made these cards that had a heading and ideas for coping skills, so she could relate back to them instead of cutting herself. Cherelle made her own set of cards instead of listening to the therapist that had headings like "Anger," "Unloved," "Shouldn't Live," 'Unwanted," "Hurt," "Hate," "Annoyed," and "Sadness." Her Therapist and I were surprised to see these subtitles.

On March 04, 2009 Cherelle's therapist stated in her note Cherelle was "a 13 year old biracial female." She continued:

> She is oriented to time, person, and place. She denies psychotic symptoms and none are noted. She is currently cutting herself on her arms, legs and abdomen on a regular basis. She self-mutilates when she feels emotionally overwhelmed. She has difficulty with hurt, anger, and sadness in an unhealthy way. She is emotionally labile. She tends to isolate and withdraw from social activities. She has difficulty sleeping and often sleeps with her mother. She has

limited social network. She verbalizes dissatisfaction with herself...'

I seriously think Cherelle should have been hospitalized at that time!!!

Not being a professional in the field of suicide awareness, I NEVER saw the warning signs. One big sign that I missed was her being bullied by the Hill Bitches (4-Block Gang), when they broke her ribs a few months prior to her death. I found out after her death that this same gang was bulling Cherelle in school, as well. I think Cherelle being bullied had a great part in her suicide.

Unfortunately, Cherelle got involved with the wrong group of friends when she returned home, and she had experimented with alcohol and marijuana, which according to the therapists, had assisted in the impact of Depression, and she was already diagnosed with Depressive Disorder and ADHD.

Cherelle started the Schenectady High School in September 2008. She was doing decent, but her grades were dropping from A's to C's and D's, which I attributed to her active social life here in Schenectady.

She was even asked to be a Student Ambassador to travel to Europe in the summer of 2009, which she really wanted to do. I was so proud of her. Since her return home she had lost approximately 45 pounds, and she looked beautiful at 130 pounds, 5' 4" tall, brown hair and brown eyes. She was a looker!!!

One day doing chin-ups on a bar that was secured between two door jams, Cherelle hit her head. As Cherelle ran and grabbed the bar, she lifted her body and feet off the ground in an upward motion above her head. Suddenly, the bar came loose and Cherelle tumbled down on her head, receiving a knot the size of a soft ball on the back on her head and had to be brought to the hospital by ambulance. I thought she was going to die; what little did I know what was in store for me a few days later…

CHAPTER 9
Doomsday

The day started like every other morning. My alarm went off and off I went to wake the children up; Cherelle was always last.

"No soggy cereal," I would say; she hated her raisin bran cereal soggy, so that always was an incentive to get her up.

"No soggy cereal, mom," she replied back, and up she went.

Cherelle ate, showered, and dressed for school, but of course missed the bus. So she called my friend for a ride and off she went to school, as usual. After school she went directly to her boyfriend's house, so I didn't know what state of mind she was in.

It was 8:30 p.m. April 2, 2009, Cherelle's curfew time, and she was never late. Cheyenne and I sat on the couch in the living room watching television, while Darrien slept in my bedroom, which was off the living room. Cherelle just then came through the front door and slammed it behind her without saying a word. I too, didn't say a word, leaving her to calm down first. She went straight to her room like any other night and turned on her music loudly.

Cheyenne and I continued to watch television for the next half an hour or so while Cherelle occasionally would come out of her safe haven and to go down to the basement to wash and dry her laundry, her weekly chore.

I sat on the couch transferring addresses from one book to another when Cherelle came out of her room and entered the living room.

"Mommy, did you call me?"

I responded, "No honey, but since you're here, here is a paper with one of your web sites on it."

"Thanks mom," she said as she headed back to her room with a smile, after grabbing a piece of gum from Cheyenne.

Soon after Cherelle's departure to her room, Cheyenne brought to my attention that Cherelle's music was louder than usual.

"Mom, could you please tell Cherelle to turn her music down. I can't hear the T.V., and she always yells at me when I ask."

"Ok honey, wait a minute, I just want to finish the last couple of these addresses.

"Ok."

Knock… Knock…

No answer on Cherelle's door.

I knock again…, again no answer.

I tried peeking through the hole in her door, but couldn't see anything.

I knocked again, this time harder and with emotion.

Finally the door cracked just enough and I saw her feet. I then tried to open the door, but it seemed to be locked. My mind was racing as I forcefully came at the door with my entire body weight to hopefully break down the door, without avail. I tried again, with no success. My daughter had passed out behind her door and I couldn't get to her.

I quickly turned around and ran through the dining room to the living room and out through the hallway to the front door landing on the front porch and yelled for help to my neighbors across the street, who were all out on the front steps chatting.

"Help me! I need a man to break down my daughter's

door! It's locked and she passed out behind her door and I can't get it open!"

As soon as a man started walking my way I yelled "Hurry up!" and turned around and ran back through the house to Cherelle's bedroom door.

I once again attempted to push on the door, but somehow the door rolled open about four inches by itself. Perplexed, but not hesitating, I pushed on the door enough so I could squeeze through. I turned around the door and my heart dropped instantly....

"You have to be kidding me!" I blurted out.

There hung my daughter by a turquoise scarf around the neck about one foot off the ground hanging in her closet.

I quickly came around behind the door to Cherelle's limp, blue body as the man came in behind me. I bent over and grabbed and lifted my daughter under her arms as I yelled, "Cut her down!" The man brought out a knife and did just that.

Without hesitation, I pulled my limp daughter's body around in half a circle and laid her flat on her back on the floor after the man made room for us. I tilted her head back and began CPR. I had asked the man if he knew CPR. Since he did not, I was on my own. I yelled for Cheyenne to call 911; however, the man had already called. They remained on the line with us until the paramedics arrived.

Puff, puff, and then compressions I thought to myself. I didn't remember how many to do, but I did them right and more than enough. After each breath there was an awful noise that Cherelle had made that I'll never forget. I worked on my daughter for at least ten to fifteen minutes before help arrived. I know for a fact that my daughter was dead when I had cut her down; unfortunately, there was no reviving her.

Cheyenne came in at one point and saw me giving Cherelle CPR, and I yelled at her to leave. I wish my poor daughter didn't have to witness such a horrible sight; it will be engraved in her memory forever.

"911 would like you to stop and see if she's breathing yet," said the man as Cheyenne was leaving the room.

"No, I won't stop; I know she's not breathing," I said with unknown composure.

Soon the Schenectady Police arrived and said that I could stop now, as the paramedics were on their way.

"I won't stop until someone pulls me off my daughter," I said.

Within minutes the paramedics arrived and with authority requested I leave the room.

The police brought me outside onto the front porch, but I yearned to be with my daughter. Suddenly I began to cough profusely and couldn't stop. It felt like I had swallowed a fly or something and couldn't clear it. Darrien, who was now awake by all the commotion and Cheyenne too, were running around the house with their heads cut off, not knowing exactly what was happening. The policemen now needed to write up their report, but I wasn't in a shape or form to give a statement, but I had to. I did my best, spitting out one word at a time through my coughing spell. When they were satisfied, they let me collect my children I had left and look for a place for them to stay while I went to the hospital with Cherelle.

I ran across the street to my neighbor's house, once again, where a group of people had collaborated on the front porch to watch all the excitement.

I asked in a quivering voice, "Could the kids stay here while I go to the hospital with Cherelle?"

Someone answered "Of course they can. You don't have to worry about them; they'll be safe. You just go be with Cherelle."

I responded: "Ok, thank you so much."

Off I went running in a daze back towards the house and up the front porch stairs two at a time. I attempted to go back into the house, but was quickly stopped by a Schenectady Police Officer who stood about five inches taller than I, who just bore down on me.

"You need to stay out here," the Police Officer said with authority.

"I need a drink. I can't stop coughing." I guess my cough must have been from giving Cherelle CPR. I had never done CPR on a real person before; I had heard that it was rough on the body.

Anyways, the Police Officer let me into the house to get my iced tea that sat on the living room table. As I approached the table, I quickly glanced around the corner of the dining room entrance and into Cherelle's room. It was a living nightmare. I felt like I was watching ER in person. The paramedics were still busy giving Cherelle CPR, and here I was told by the Schenectady Police Officer a few moments earlier that

Cherelle was "Okay." I was shocked; my heart fell into my stomach with a loud thud. I couldn't believe it; my daughter was officially DEAD!!!

The Police Officer had called for me, but I ignored him as I watched in horror as the paramedics probed my daughter with pumps and tubes. Soon enough, I was grabbed by the arm and quickly removed from view. I was once again brought outside onto the front porch to complete missed items on the police report.

Finally, it was time to go to the hospital.

"Do you have a ride to the hospital", one of the Officer's inquired

I said "No, I don't".

They offered to give me a ride in the police car. I accepted.

They escorted me to a police car that sat about two car lengths behind the ambulance. I staggered as I walked as if I were drunk, looking behind me as I walked as if Cherelle was going to run out the house after me. I made it to the Police car within a few minutes. I climbed into the back seat and waited for my daughter to be brought out. It felt like forever. I tried to escape this madness and run to Cherelle's side, but the

Police car's back doors locked and I couldn't get out. I sat there with tears streaming down my face. There was no stopping them. I felt useless. I needed to be with my daughter, but they wouldn't let me. I hated them for that, but was grateful they were there to help.

Finally, the time has come. It felt like forever. Cherelle's body was brought out. Several medical personal surrounded her. I watched through tear-filled eyes as they rushed her into the ambulance. Off we went in minutes towards Ellis Hospital.

I sat in the back of the police car and just starred at the ambulance's red lights flashing in front of my face. We passed every red light without stopping. I just sat their racing in my own thoughts.

"I can't believe this."

"Why Cherelle," I mumbled.

"I love you sooooooooo much."

"Please come back."

"Please………live…" I trailed off as unstoppable salty tears took over.

I prayed that the trip to the hospital would never end, because I knew that my daughter was dead and the 'hospital' just meant that it would be final. They would tell me the inevitable, "We're sorry; we did everything we could do."

The trip to the hospital eventually did end. I was escorted by the police to the Register's office. How at a time like this could I sit long enough to register my daughter? I needed to be with her, DAMN IT!! They just took her insurance card and that was it. Thank God.

"May I use your phone to call my mother?" I asked in a quivering voice.

"Sure, use this one." She set me up with a phone a few feet away.

I dialed her number cautiously.

"Hello," it was my mother.

"Mommy, Cherelle hung herself."

"What?"

"Cherelle hung herself."

"Where are you?"

"Ellis Hospital."

"Ok. I'll be right there."

As soon as I got off the phone, the nurse introduced me to this petite lady with soft white hair who wore a black and white outfit.

"This is our Chaplin," the nurse stated.

I screamed, "NO, SHE'S NOT DEAD!"

They said, "No honey, we always have the Chaplin sit with the family when their family member is in respiratory distress."

I hesitated, then through my tears said, "Oh… ooh ok."

The nurse led us to a small private room around the back hall behind the nurse's station. The Chaplin and I were alone in this room. I could hear myself breathe, but I couldn't sit still.

"Can I use the phone? I need to call Cherelle's dad."

"Sure honey, I'll dial it for you," replied the soft-spoken women.

I hesitated with each number, as I spit out all seven digits. I placed the receiver to my ear. The telephone rang. I was relieved to hear that he didn't shut his phone off yet for the night.

Finally, I heard a familiar voice on the other end of the telephone line.

"Hello."

"Dee," I said crying hysterically, "Cherelle hung herself."

"What?" "What are you talking about?" he said confused.

"I said Cherelle hung herself tonight, and I think she's not gonna make it!"

"Hold up, where are you?"

"Ellis Hospital."

"I'll be right there," was the last thing I heard him say as he hung up.

"Can I call one more person? I need to call Kim, my best friend."

"Sure honey, call anyone you need to."

Again I spit out the numbers, as she pressed them into the telephone.

"Kim."

"What's wrong?"

"Cherelle hung herself," I cried.

"What?"

"Cherelle hung herself, and I think she's dead!"

"Lisa, where are you?"

"Ellis Hospital."

"I'll be right there."

Kim only lived a few blocks away from the hospital, so I knew that she would be the first one to the hospital to comfort me. She arrived approximately seven minutes after hanging up with her. I saw her coming and met her in the waiting room. We hugged and held each other for a minute until we were led back to my private room once again.

Kim was as nervous as I was for the verdict that we knew we were about to receive. We sat as close as we could to each other without actually sitting on top of one another.

"Kim, what am I gonna do if she dies?" I whined.

"Don't talk like that. She'll pull through".

"I hope so, Kim."

We sat holding hands, squeezing each other as tight as we could while Kim's other arm was around me holding me tight against her body. Suddenly, the private room door started to open. All three of us glanced towards the door as Kim and I froze in our tears.

It was the doctor. There he stood, a Chinese doctor not much taller than me dressed in his doctor's gown. He spoke in a calm tone of voice, but I wasn't ready to hear the words he was about to say. He didn't have to say anything, his eyes said it all. The doctor introduced himself then said the inevitable….

"I'm sorry; we did everything we could….." That's all I heard. Everything else sounded like mumble jumble.

"Nooooooooooooooo", I screamed simultaneously with Kim. I screamed from the bottom of my lungs and couldn't stop. The entire hospital must have heard us.

"Kim, oh my God, Kim, What am I going to do?"

"She's DEAD, Kim, she DEAD!" I cried trailing off.

All at once I remembered Dee was coming, so I jumped up and went to the waiting room door's window. Soon Dee came rushing in. I too met him in the waiting room and brought him into the private area.

"Dee, she's DEAD!" I cried without hesitation.

"Nooooo…" he moaned as he placed his hand over his face and frantically paced around.

"Why?", he questioned me

"I don't know, Dee", I said.

Not knowing quite what to say or do next I jumped up, once again and headed for the waiting door window and stated to Dee, "I need to wait for my mom".

Soon enough my mother arrived at the hospital, but she was not alone, my sister Debi was with her, as well. Again I met my company in the waiting room, but couldn't wait to get my family in the private room before telling them the horrific news.

I flung open the door and ran to them. I exploded; yelling "SHE'S DEAD MOMMY, SHE'S DEAD!!! Both of my mother and sisters faces' turned white and had no expression; tears began to flow down their faces.

I led them back to the private room to have some privacy with me in this time of sorrow. The Chaplin, Kim and I sat back down in the same spot and my mom and Dee sat at an angle to my left, while Debi stood in the doorway.

"I just can't believe she did this", Debi said "Cheyenne would have been the last one I thought would have done this."

"Cheyenne?" I said perplexed, "it wasn't Cheyenne; it was Cherelle."

"Cherelle, Nooooo, not Cherelle…." My sister screamed, as her knees buckled and went down towards the floor, but the Chaplin rushed to her and caught her.

At the same time, my mother screamed as well: "Cherelle…No…..Not Cherelle…." Dee wrapped his arms around her to console her.

Just before everyone arrived, a nurse came in and said that we could view Cherelle's body as soon as they cleaned her up. We all sat quietly and cried in our own sorrow until they came to retrieve us. We then followed the nurse like baby ducklings following their mother. My mind was racing; thoughts of what Cherelle might look like bounced through my head. The room fast approached. It was time to go in.

I stood outside the ER door for a minute before entering Cherelle's room. I took a deep breath and closed my eyes and took that first step; then I opened up my eyes to see my beautiful baby laying there on the ER bed. She was so peaceful. I walked over to her right side and busted out crying. There was no stopping my tears; they were coming from a broken faucet. Her dark brown hair was pulled back in a ponytail, which was all muffled up. Her beautiful brown eyes were closed, and her pale skin was cold and clammy to the touch.

I stood next to her for a couple minutes, then I sat down next to Cherelle in the cold metal chair that the nurse offered me. I just couldn't stop kissing her cold, cold face. I also hung onto her hand tightly, and she seemed to be holding mine too.

"Can I take her rings and earrings off?" I asked the nurse politely.

"Sure you can," she replied.

I removed all three of her rings and placed them onto my hands as if they were priceless diamonds. Along with the rings, I removed a hair tie from Cherelle's right wrist that she always wore. She'd say, "You never know when you need a hair tie." I placed this hair tie on my wrist and will never take it off for as long as I live.

My mom, sister, Kim, and Cherelle's dad, Dee, along with the Chaplin were also in the ER room saying our last goodbyes and asking "Why? Why Cherelle? Why would you do this?" This question, of course, will never be answered.

It just so happened that Cherelle's papa recently had surgery on his hand and was in Ellis Hospital on a different floor. My mother had left the ER room where Cherelle lay to go notify my father of this unfortunate tragedy. He was heartbroken.

Within ten minutes my mother returned with my father in a Geri chair. He was dressed in a hospital gown, of course. He was saddened by the site of my daughter, but he kept his composure. Cherelle and my father had a special bond between them. Cherelle loved my father with all her heart and soul, and it was going to kill my father sooner than later. She always had this hardy laugh around him that used to make her belly shake. That's where she got the name Relly Belly, 'Relly' for short.

We all spent quality time with Cherelle's body, but Dee and I had to leave to go home to tell my other children that their sister was gone. I didn't want to leave. I just wanted to hold onto my daughter and never let her go. It hurt so badly. Dee made me leave. He pretty much dragged me out. I said my last goodbyes to Cherelle and everyone else and off we went to locate Dee's car.

Dee parked in the ER parking lot. We found his car quickly and got in, Dee behind the wheel and I in the passenger seat, we went toward my home. Kim was to meet us there shortly, too. I dreaded what was to come.

"What do we say to the kids?" I asked curious about his response.

"Just tell them that Cherelle didn't make it," Dee said without hesitation.

"Ok," I mumbled.

I was quiet for a long portion of the ride home, not able to find the right words to speak to Dee. I didn't know exactly what Cherelle thought about before she killed herself, so it was hard to explain to Dee what happened that night. I just sat there running through my own thoughts.

"I'll stay at Kim's for now," I said breaking the silence.

Ten minutes later we pulled up in front of our house and our neighbor directed us to the other neighbor's house where my children spent night. The neighbors met us outside on the sidewalk with open arms.

"She's dead," I wailed.

"Oh honey," said the neighbor as she wrapped her arms around me.

"What am I going to do?" I sniffed.

"Let me go tell the kids," I said.

"Come on, I'll show you where they are," and I followed her.

Cheyenne and Darrien were in the back bedroom wide awake waiting for our return. I walked in and they searched my face for answers. I couldn't hold back as tears rolled down my face.

"Cherelle didn't make it," I cried.

Cheyenne went hysterical.

"I want my sissy," cried Cheyenne over and over, as Darrien just buried his head into my side and cried. It was a horrible sight. I never saw children in so much emotional pain before.

After about five minute of crying and consoling the children, Dee and I took the kids to Kim's truck, while I went into the house to retrieve a few outfits for the next couple of days to stay over Kim's house.

Once again, Kim was my life-saver. She invited my now little family to stay with her at her home for as long as we needed to. When it comes to friends, Kim was the truest.

Cheyenne, Darrien, and I arrived with Kim at her home. We settled the children into their spots for the night, but only Darrien could sleep, due to his sleeping medication. Kim and I just sat on the couch and talked.

Cheyenne couldn't sleep either. She tossed and turned all night, so she stayed up with us as well. We stayed up until approximately four in the morning. We all needed some type of sleep, so Cheyenne and I laid our heads down on the couch; sleep was hard to find. It was like finding a needle in a haystack. Cheyenne was the strong one, I was not. I continued to cry throughout the night, sometimes to the point of hyperventilating. Kim kept trying to calm me down. It didn't seem real; this life just can't be real! My baby girl was gone.

CHAPTER 10
Funeral Arrangements

The Friday after Cherelle died was Joe's (Darrien's Dad's) five year anniversary of his suicide; it that strange or what? Anyways, Dee (Cherelle's dad), my sister Debi and I had made an appointment to meet with the funeral director at Lights Funeral Home to make Cherelle's funeral arrangements. I couldn't believe it--funeral arrangements?

I was anxiously waiting for my sister Debi to pick Dee and me up from Kim's house to drive us to the Funeral Home. Lights Funeral Home was expecting us. They led us to a small open room with a large table with four chairs around it. We each took a chair. We all introduced ourselves and told our story briefly to the Funeral Director. The man was very kind and sympathetic. He explained exactly what a funeral entailed. We all listened intensely, but I couldn't do anything but cry. At one point, the Funeral Director mentioned that we could apply to Social Services for assistance, because I was on Social Security. Disability

Insurance could get 75% of the funeral services paid for. WOW! That would be wonderful, since our bill was looking like $6080.00.

We sat there at the Funeral Home for hours discussing whom we should choose for a Pastor to lead Cherelle's services. The Funeral Director had a young, vibrant one in mind, so we went with him. Then we had to decide whether to have her wake at the funeral home verses a church, where there would be more room to accommodate a large crowd that a young girl would draw in, especially being the fourth suicide in Schenectady. She was one of four suicides in Schenectady High School.

We also sat there and looked through books and chose flowers for her casket that read "Daughter" and "Sister."

"Pink and purple," I cried. "They were her favorite colors besides blue."

Then my sister chose one that read "Niece" and "Cousins" and then we chose one more for our parents that read "Granddaughter." They were all so beautiful. We also chose memory cards and a Guest book with butterflies flying free on it. Then came the tough part: the casket.

"Pink," I said. "She has to have pink."

They didn't have a cheap pink one in the building so they had one sent over and we could come back in a couple hours to view it. It was perfect, exactly what I wanted: a beautiful light pink casket for my beautiful girl.

In the meantime, Debi and I had gone back to my house to pick out just the right dress for Cherelle while we waited for the casket to arrive at the funeral home. Man, that was one of the hardest thing to do. I wanted her to look just right. I had about seven dresses to choose from. I let my sister help chose the very best one because I just couldn't do it alone. I kept breaking down.

At one point, when I was supposed to be getting her undergarments, Debi found me all curled up in Cherelle's bed crying hysterically, and I wouldn't leave. I just wanted my daughter back.

I regained my composure eventually and collected the necessary items the funeral home requested from us, and we returned to the funeral home where we met back up with Dee. It turned out that we still needed a sweater or something to go over Cherelle's chest due to the autopsy that was performed in the hospital. I forgot all about the autopsy.

We wrapped up our session and were satisfied with our decisions for the day. We now placed everything that dealt with Cherelle's funeral in the hands of Lights Funeral Home, and what a relief that was. After leaving the funeral home, we went to Wal-Mart and bought her a brown sweater, which was perfect and returned it to the funeral home some time later.

Back to Kim house I went. Time seemed to stand still since Cherelle passed. I remained at Kim's house for two days. I had a lot of support from friends and family while I was there. I even had my children's Counseling Agencies involved in my support, along with support for the children. The children seem to be stronger than I was.

I was anxious to get home, but before I did that I decided to stay with my parent's until after Cherelle's funeral services were over. Cheyenne and I stayed at my parent's home, while Darrien remained at Kim's house. He enjoyed Kim's house more since Kim has a son for him to play with and there is really nothing for him to do at Grandma's, but mope around and cry, if that.

We had to go back to the funeral home on Saturday to review Cherelle's obituary that was going to run in Sunday's *Schenectady Gazette* newspaper. It read: Cherelle Allie Clarke, 14, of Schenectady, passed away tragically on Thursday evening April 2, 2009, at her home.

Born on November 25, 1994 in Schenectady, NY, she was the beloved daughter of Lisa J. Seymour and DeVaughn E. Clarke. Cherelle attended grade school in Schenectady until transferring for middle school in Burnt Hills. She most recently returned to the Schenectady School District where she was attending ninth grade at Schenectady High School. Throughout her school years she was a cheerleader, member of the drama club and choir, and participated in various sports. Cherelle most recently was selected for the Student Ambassador Program.

She was a dynamic young lady with many friends and interests. She enjoyed swimming, horseback riding, singing, shopping, drawing, designing, music, arts and crafts, going to Broadway shows, was an accomplished writer and published poet, volunteered with the Lake Desolation Fire Department, and most of all enjoyed spending time with her family and friends. Those close to her will remember her as a beautiful, caring, empathetic, and loving girl.

Besides her parents, survivors include her sister Cheyenne Clarke; brother, Darrien Corley-- I won't list the other people to protect their identities.

Anyways, it was a beautiful write up but very sad. At this point I still couldn't believe that my daughter was gone. The Funeral Director had given us four large poster boards and I already had two smaller ones to place Cherelle's picture's on to display at the time of the wake. So I had to dig out all of Cherelle's pictures from childhood to when she passed away, and was that a lot.

Sunday Debi, Cheyenne, Shauna, Sarah, Brianna, my sister, Sherri, and I were extremely busy producing six poster boards of Cherelle. Some of the boards were of her alone, some of her with family and others were of her with friends. They all turned out GREAT!

Back at my parent's home I waited for that dreadful day of Monday April 06, 2009 – the wake. I woke up on that morning to the Schenectady Gazette Newspaper laying on my parent's table. The headline story was about Cherelle, and it read: "Student Plagued by Bullies before Suicide." I couldn't believe it. This was the beginning of Cherelle's publicity.

CHAPTER 11
The Services

Viewing hours for Cherelle's wake were from 4:00 p.m. – 7:00 p.m., with a service at 7:00 p.m. However, the family could view the body at 12:00 p.m. and 3:00 p.m., and that's just what I did. Debi picked me up from my parent's house, and we met Dee at the Lights Funeral Home. I started to cry before I even got out of the car, but that was to be expected. I slowly walked up to the front door and rang the bell next to the double doors. Soon one of the doors flew open up by one of the Funeral Directors. I walked through it and up the two steps towards the room that held my daughter. I approached the room, leaving Debi behind and entered it on an exhale.

There she was; at the far end of the room lay my first born, my most beautiful, precious daughter, lying there in her pretty light pink casket. Dee was already in the room about seven feet from the casket when I entered. I started to bawl and my knees were weak. My sister caught up to me by now and we walked to see Cherelle up close together and personal.

Cherelle lay there so peaceful. Her hair looked beautiful, as it was straightened and pulled slightly forward around her ears and she had bangs cut just above her eye brows. We chose a turquoise and brown flowery pattern dress with a ¾ sleeve brown button-down sweater. Cherelle wore her new, one week old, Vogue glasses, with 14k gold hoop earrings and a necklace from her Grandmother that read on the reverse side: "I will always be at your side." Also one of my best friends, Heidi, also gave Cherelle a Sterling Silver necklace to hold in her hands while she lay so peacefully in her casket.

I couldn't take my eyes off her. They felt as if the had been glued down with super glue. I touched my baby's cheek. It was hard and cold as ice. It gave me chills, but I didn't pull away. This was my daughter, my first born. WHY!!! I continued to stand there with tears continually rolling down my face wiping away my makeup.

I sat with my daughter, Cherelle, for the entire hour, than Lights Funeral Home took Cherelle to the church on Broadway in Schenectady that'swhere we had all decided to have the 'wake', since it was large and would hold more people.

After we left Cherelle at Lights Funeral Home before she was brought to the Church, Debi and I headed back to my parent's home to get ready for the 'wake'. We had to be there by 3:00 pm to get in our family hour alone with Cherelle and all her flowers.

We arrived at the Church a few minutes after 3:00 pm. Debi and I walked in together this time at a steady pace. It was like day-ay-vue; Cherelle, of course, remained in the same position as I had seen her a few hours previously, however this time, there were many large flower arrangements everywhere. Dee's and my beautiful pink and purple bouquet of flowers that read 'Daughter' rested on top of her light pink casket. The other bouquets from her sister and brother, my sister, and her cousins and her Grandparents lay around and in front of the casket. Several other flower arrangements from people of unknown origin also were distributed around the casket in such a beautiful way. Lights Funeral Home did an awesome job.

My niece, Brianna, was producing a DVD of picture of Cherelle for birth to the present to play on the two televisions that the Church offered on both sides of the walls in the room that Cherelle was in. But things weren't going so well and they lost all their information initially, but they did redo it and brought the DVD's during the 'wake', which were just beautiful.

I wasn't strong at all and I cried for the entire hour before people started coming in to give their respects. Dee was stronger than me, but he too had his moments.

So much for looking nice for everyone; I dressed in black pelted pants with a white fitted button down blouse that hung over my hips, with black two-inch heels. I must have looked like a train wreck from all my crying by the time the wake opened for people to view Cherelle. Oh well; that's life.

My parents sat in the front row, close enough to where they could glance at Cherelle when they wanted too. It was horrible to see my father's eyes build up with tears as he came to give Cherelle his respects. I wish there was something that I could have done to bring back Papa's little Relly Belly.

My mother cried, as expected. I went up with her to view Cherelle's body. She touched her face with her hand.

"She's so cold."

"I know," I said.

"Doesn't she look nice," I cried.

"She looks beautiful honey. She is a beautiful girl," my mother answered.

We held each other tight as we touched Cherelle's cold and clammy face.

It was time for the public to view my baby. From 4:00 p.m. to 7:00 p.m. there were non-stop people coming in. The Schenectady Police Department was even on the premises to control the crowd. Friends of mine and my family's and Dee and his family came to console us, along with strangers that I never met. I had never witnessed so many children in so much emotional pain than I saw that night.

That night was a blur for me, like I had tunnel vision or something and only Cherelle was in my view. People kept coming up to me all night long to hug and kiss me, but all I wanted was be alone with my baby girl.

"Leave me alone," I wanted to say to everyone, but instead I thanked everyone for coming.

Nothing anyone of these people could say could make me feel any better, or for that matter, bring back my daughter.

I must have cried most of the night. One would have thought that I would have run out of tears, but they never stopped. Darrien, on the other hand, cried a little bit but never came up to the casket to pay his respects. He never got closure. He remained in the distance as far from the casket as we would allow.

Dee was a great means of support for me during this time of sorrow. We became much closer than we had ever been in the years past. It was nice to see that we could count on each other when times got hard.

Cheyenne, on the other hand, was hysterical. She cried so hard she hyperventilated. She did, on the other hand, frequent the casket, which would upset her more, but she insisted on it.

"I want my sister," she would scream.

"I want my sister," is all she would say!

Her father and I both, along with relatives, took turns to console her, but at one point in the night we had to send one of the counselors that we'd been working with out to the store to buy some Melatonin to calm her down, because she was so upset that it was making her sick.

The Church had provided two nurses in front of Cherelle's casket to hold large boxes of tissues for those in need. They were also there to protect Cherelle from people touching her.

Minutes turned into hours as people continued non-stop to pay their respects to my beautiful girl. There were a lot of young people that came in, too. I didn't recognize a lot them; they must have known Cherelle from the Schenectady High School.

One point in the night I was introduced to the Mayor of the City of Schenectady. He had come out to give his condolences and speak at Cherelle's service. I couldn't believe it; Cherelle brought the Mayor to her wake. Wow!!! Go Cherelle!!

Seven o'clock came quickly; it was that time, time to close the casket. That was the hardest part for me. It meant FOREVER GONE!!! I didn't want them to close it. I didn't want my baby to get closed into a dark box by herself. I kept kissing her, and I wouldn't let her go.

"No," I yelled, as my knees buckled and Dee caught me dragging me away from the casket in order for them to close it up. It was horrifying. I needed to see my baby one last time, but they wouldn't let me. Dee sat me down in my seat, and I waited for the service to start.

It was time for the Pastor to start his service. The music began to roar and the choir began to sing. It was just beautiful. The Church helpers passed out pamphlets to everyone in the church that read in bold letters at the top "Celebration of Life" For Cherelle Allie Clarke.

Within this pamphlet read:

> Processional, Pray of Comfort, Scripture readings: Old Testament Scripture and New Testament Scripture, Choir, Special Reading (by my sister Debra Ryan), Favorite Song (Amazing Grace), Poem "I'm Me," written by Cherelle (read by Dee Clarke), Words of Expression, Reading of Sympathy Cards/Obituary, Words of Expression

LISA SEYMOUR

(Lisa Seymour), Choir, Eulogy, Services Entrusted To (Lights Funeral Home), Recessional.

Cherelle's father, Dee, read one of her poems at the service that was published in a poetry book and can be found on poetry.com titled "I'm me" and it goes like this:

Sometimes I act childish like
my brother and sister.
I always wish I could see them
more and more.
But I know all I have to do is
pick up the phone and call.
When I'm mad people call me my brother.
When I'm really jumpy and happy
people call me my sister.
But I know that I'm not my brother, and I'm
not my sister, I'm me.

I also read one of her poems at the service titled, "This is My Life"

Cherelle.
Intelligent, amazing, caring and loving.
Daughter of Lisa Seymour and DeVaughn Clarke.
Lover of Animals, purses, and jewelry.
Who feels stupid at times, scared while watching scary movies, and sad at funerals.
Who finds happiness in my own room, a room full of animals, a beautiful tropical island.
Who needs hugs, my family, and the water.
Who gives my mom hugs, my dad kisses, and animals kindness.
Who fears scary movies, being alone at night, and dying.
Who would like to see Hawaii, my cousin Devine one last time, and all the different kinds of dogs and cats in the world.
Who enjoys watching TV, singing, playing on the computer, and scrap-booking.
Who likes to wear camies with pajama pants, jewelry, and sneakers.
Resident of New York.
Clarke.

After the recessional the Pastor got the church hopping. Music was blaring, people were jumping all around; it was wonderful. Cherelle would have wanted this kind of wake. The pastor was trying to get the word out 'That the Devil will not win--we will win! That suicide is not the way out."

The Pastor got his word out to his audience of approximately three hundred people, young and old alike. Some were smiling, some were crying, some had no expression at all. I on the other hand was swept up in all the commotion. It was amazing. How I yearned for Cherelle to be there to witness this wonderful experience, but she was there in Spirit.

The church service was absolutely beautiful. Cherelle's posters hung beautifully in the front entrance, so when you first walked in you noticed them. Then, thanks to Brianna, Cherelle's picture DVD's played up until the service started. All involved did a wonderful job, but it all came to an end. I didn't want it to end. That meant closure for Cherelle, and I didn't want that yet.

I rode back to my parent's house with my sister Debi, her family and my children. It was a rough night, and I was exhausted. We had to be up early to be at the funeral home by 11:00 am to place special items in

Cherelle's casket that we wanted her to take with her, so I went to bed early.

Morning came quickly. I wasn't at all ready for this-- to bury my daughter! She was only 14 year old. I woke up, but not willingly. I knew I had to get up and start my day or I'd miss out on my daughter's funeral.

Another story about a "String of Suicides Prompts Awareness Forum," appeared in the Paper. They stated within the article that the, "4th victim recalled as 'Bubbliest kid.'" Cherelle's suicide has sparked the community's awareness of these last four suicides of the Schenectady High School students and the need for help.

My sister Debi once again came to pick me up and brought me to the Funeral Home, along with my other middle sister, Sherri. We arrived approximately twenty minutes later; Dee and his girlfriend met us there.

Once again, Cherelle was in that same room as she was in before, that dreadful room. It hurt just as much to look at Cherelle this time as it did the first time. But this time there were no pretty flowers, well maybe just a few. The rest had been delivered to the grave site already. How sad is that?

Anyways, there sat a table to the right of the casket with all different types of things on it, like her white bear that sat one night outside our front door, four different glass mirror figurines and fake flowers. Also on this table were three stuffed animals, one large, two small, Aunt Sherri's jar of shells, a few letters from her friends and a Penguin stuffed animal that we all wrote something special to Cherelle on. Dee and I chose pretty much everything but the glass figurines, fake flowers and two of the stuffed animals to remain with Cherelle on top of her grave.

I placed each item in Cherelle's casket with precision. It seemed to me like each item had it own proper place. I cried as I placed each piece in. Aunt Sherri's shells sat next to her left wrist as Hailey's 'cross' hung from her hands, since Heidi's necklace was placed around her neck, because I had requested that the one with the saying on the back of it be returned to me in memory of my daughter, along with the hoop earrings, as well. I placed 'Tynni's' letter next to her right upper arm and the letter with the small stuffed animal I placed near her right forearm. The Penguin I nestled up in her left arm pit area, as if she was holding it.

My sisters, Dee and his girlfriend, along with the Funeral Director were all looking at pictures of Cherelle and books that she had made, but not me, I spent every last minute with my daughter. I never wanted to leave her side, but I knew our hour was dwindling down and coming to an end, and it did.

I couldn't let go of Cherelle. I grabbed at my daughter like she was drowning. Dee tried to drag me away, but I squirmed away from his grip and ran back to the casket where my daughter dwelled.

"No… Cherelle… No…," I screamed.

"You can't take her," I continued.

"Get her out of here," the Funeral Director ordered.

"OK…," Dee said heading towards me.

Dee snatched me up as I was just about pass out. He dragged me out through the doors as I tried to grab the wall jam, but did not succeed. Out the front doors I went and into the front seat of my sister's car. I sat to wait for Cherelle's body to be brought out to the hearse to drive to the Parkview Cemetery where Cherelle was to be buried. We were able to follow the hearse to the cemetery without a problem.

I was so anxiously sitting there in the car like I could have exploded. If I could have I would have opened up the door and darted back into the building to Cherelle's side, but I knew the door was locked and they wouldn't let me in. Suddenly the doors opened up and out rolled Cherelle's casket with a few men to lift her into the hearse. Up and in she went as tears rolled down my face and my hand was pressed against the window.

"Cherelle...," I said softly through my tears.

"Cherelle, come back...."

The hearse's doors were closed and the Funeral Directors got into the front of the hearse and off it went towards Parkview Cemetery, which was less than a mile away from the Funeral Home. We pulled out directly behind the hearse, and Dee trailed behind us.

We arrived shortly after 12:00 pm to Parkview Cemetery, where Cherelle's body was going to be laid to rest. We pulled up and it looked as if no one was there to say Goodbye to my beautiful baby girl. I was really disappointed and saddened by the sight, but then I was mistakin when I looked around and there was a large gathering down the road for Cherelle's funeral.

It was a brisk, cloudy and windy day that my baby was going to be buried in the cold ground. I wasn't happy at all, actually, I was a mess! Dee was doing better than I, but again, he had his moments. We all watched as Cherelle's body was removed from the hearse then it was time to make our way to the burial site. Cherelle's casket led the way, then Dee and I followed next then the group of people followed suit. Everyone grabbed a place around the casket, with family in front at the top of Cherelle's head. I could barely see out of my eyes, no less walk or stand. Cheyenne and Darrien stood next to me near the top of Cherelle's casket, with Dee next to Cheyenne and Grandma next to Darrien. I have never cried so much; I was so weak I thought I was going to pass out.

It was time for the service to start, which was short, but beautiful. The Pastor gathered everyone around and we all said the "Lord's Prayer," had a moment of silence then we all went into the field where there were 100 pink and purple balloons to be let loose in memory of Cherelle. The one good thing about this windy day is the balloons went sailing away south towards New York

City to Broadway – for her Broadway shows she liked so much.

I, of course, snuck back to Cherelle's casket again and the Funeral Director caught me. It was alright though; I just had to be careful not to knock the casket and myself into the already dug hole. I stood there for a while with Kim and Heidi, and then Dee came over. Eventually this all had to end, I had to leave my little girl here and go home without her. How do you do that? I didn't know.

"Everyone, can I have your attention, Please," the Funeral Director barked.

"Lisa and Dee would like you all to know that they are have a get-together serving lunch at the Church on Broadway. The same Church as the wake. So please, join them right after the funeral. Thank you and thank you for coming."

The funeral ended, but again I didn't want to go until I saw Cheyenne crying hard again.

"I want my sister," she roared.

"I want my sister."

I couldn't help but feel terrible for her. I had to get her out of there. Then I saw the Cemetery workers taking down Cherelle's equipment and getting her ready to be lifted into the ground. I couldn't watch that and I especially couldn't let my children see that. I had to get out of there and NOW!

"Debi, come on, let's go, hurry up," I said rushing Debi.

"What," Debi said confused.

"They're starting to bury Cherelle and we need to get out of here now. Cheyenne doesn't need to see this," I said stuttering over my words.

"Oooh, OK, let's go," Debi responded as she jumped into her car and off we went towards the church on Broadway.

The church on Broadway was same Church we had frequented the night before, but this time, no Cherelle. When we arrived the tables were full of food from family and friends and different people in the community. It was wonderful to see people come together like this when people are in need. My sister Debi's friends put in a lot of time and effort to make Cherelle's party a success and I thank them both for it. They know who they are.

The turn-out for the party was great. A lot of friends and family came to support us in this time of sorrow. I just wasn't in a partying mood or in an eating mood, for that matter. I haven't eaten more than two halves of a sandwich in the last six days and really didn't feel like starting to now. So I just had a cup of coffee and tried to talk with some of my old childhood friends in the back of the room.

We had put up all six of Cherelle's picture boards again so people could look a little closer at the pictures if they wanted to. The party lasted a good 2 – 2 ½ hours. I tried hard to keep my composure throughout this period of time, but failed frequently, especially when the Funeral Director brought in a bag full of Cherelle's goodies, which included two locks of her hair, the jewelry she wore in the casket, a pack of memory cards, and the Guest book.

After the gathering, my little family headed back to my parent's home, this time including Darrien. We didn't even get to stay that night when my mother and I got into an argument. The stress of the situation was too much for us to handle and we took it out on each other.

It was a shame, because we really needed each other in this time of sorrow.

Cherelle's death drew a lot of attention from the media and from our City's Mayor, who spoke at Cherelle's wake, and the community even started a Suicide Forum that was being held the same night of Cherelle's funeral; however, I wasn't in any shape to appear, so I did not go, but I heard it was really informative.

CHAPTER 12
Coming Back to Reality

Wednesday, the day after my baby was buried; I was back in my own house again, with both Cheyenne and Darrien by my side. It was hard, but I felt comfortable with it, and I asked the children what they wanted to do and they both said, "Go home;" so we did.

It was hard not to cry being in the house where I found my daughter less than a week ago, but I found myself crying and frequenting Cherelle's room, wrapping myself up in her blankets and crying myself to sleep. Only I cried, my other children never shed any tears.

My friends Heidi, Russ and Spring were a great support to me during this hard time. One of them was always there when I needed someone. I wasn't left alone for the first few weeks after Cherelle's death and Heidi, Russ and Spring continued to support me as much as they could afterwards. I also had a lot of clinicians coming into my home to check on me and my children on a daily basis. It was great to know so many people cared.

I attended a Suicide Forum the second weekend after Cherelle's passing. I just went to see what it was like, but instead I ended up spilling out my heart to a full crowd of people. I had brought Cherelle's picture with me and held it tight as I spoke the words about Cherelle and her death and the warning signs of suicide and what you as a parent need to look for; you don't have to be a professional anymore to see the signs and symptoms. I had the audience roaring and clapping. It made me feel great, like I got my point across. I also attended another Suicide Forum a few days prior to this one but spoke only briefly.

There was a so-called "Suicide List" that I was told that Cherelle was on. No one knows where this so-called list generated from, but I wish I found out.

The pain of missing my daughter was so unbearable that medication and regular counseling wasn't working. Northeast Parent & Child Society had noticed my suffering as well, and I was really making people and the professionals concerned; they all thought I, too, was going to commit suicide, so they referred me to Haven, a Grieving Center. It was the best thing that anyone could have done for me. The lady I spoke to on a weekly basis was so sensitive and knowledgeable about death that she really eased my fears about where Cherelle is and she listened to what I had to say, stupid or not.

One thing I do speak upon at Haven is that I believe that Cherelle is a Spirit now and she is around us. I have attended Suicide Survivors Groups, both in Albany and in Schenectady and several people also have this same belief that their loved ones are still around and that they do certain things that shows that they are still there and these are called "Winks."

Well, I have had quite a few winks from Cherelle. One in particular time was when I was shopping at Wal-Mart in the towel section a few days after Cherelle's passing. I reached up onto the top shelf and suddenly something grabbed onto my metal bracelets (bracelets that were Cherelle's that I just got out of her bedroom). I slowly reached forward and grabbed a hold of what I realized was a shell angel magnet, but to my surprise when I looked at it closer, it was Cherelle's birth stone. I truly believe that it was a sign from Cherelle letting me know that she is now an angel now.

Another wink from Cherelle happened on May 27, 2009, when my mother and I were sitting on the couch. Out of the blue, my mother had stated how nice the shelf that was built into the wall looked. So I stood up and pointed out all my children's projects, dried flowers, and cards that the shelf held on it. Then suddenly I spotted a card stuck behind one of Cheyenne's ceramic projects. I slowly pulled it out and couldn't believe my eyes. It was a Hallmark recordable Mother's Day card from, no one else, but you guessed it, Cherelle. Now Mother's Day had just passed, mind you. Anyways, when I opened up the card her voice was sweet and clear as ever and blared "You're the best mom ever! I love you!"

My heart dropped when I heard her voice and tears came rushing in as I gasped for air. My mother told me to sit down. I did. I eventually called Hallmark to see if I could get new batteries or something to savor the beautiful words, but they said no. The card had a shelf life of two years and over five years had gone by now. I believe that Cherelle wanted me to find this card with her voice on it around Mother's Day. This was priceless, so I had her voice recorded onto a CD ten times and now have it for life.

CHAPTER 13
Moving on...

Well, my luck continued to pan out towards the bad side. I did apply to Social Services like the Funeral Director had suggested, but of course I was denied because we chose a plot on top of the hill where the sun can shine on top of Cherelle, instead of in the woods where the Social Service plots rest. We didn't know that where the plot laid made a difference. So we got stuck with a $6080.00 bill. However, the Funeral Home did give us off some of the payment because she was a child, and it happened so tragically and my girlfriend, Spring, opened up a "Cherelle Clarke Fund" that brought in $1500.00 towards funeral costs.

Not only do I have great friends who help out, but Grace Memorial also did their part. They donated the entire headstone for Cherelle, with her picture on it and even paid for the digging the foundation at the cemetery. Wow, I cried when I heard this. Her stone reads:

IN LOVING MEMORY
CHERELLE ALLIE CLARKE
(RELLY)
NOV. 25, 1994 to APRIL 2, 2009

No one will ever know why Cherelle killed herself. I can always ask why, but it will never be answered. All I do know now that I've gone through all the Suicide Awareness Training is that I now I can see the signs clearly screaming at me, such as Cherelle being bullied, losing a lot of weight, losing of a friend, fighting with a boyfriend, depression, talking about suicide, losing her step-dad and friends to suicide. If only I saw the signs I may have saved her life.

CHAPTER 14
Signs of Suicide

Over 32,000 people in the US die by suicide every year. Approximately 80 people die every day, with 1500 attempts to do so Two to three times as many females attempt suicide compared to males. Suicide is the 5th leading cause of death among 5–14 year olds and 3rd among 15–24 year olds. The following are warning signs of suicide distributed by The American Foundation for Suicide Prevention:

- Withdraw from friends and/or social activities
- Experience noticeable changes in overall behavior (e.g., unexpected rage or anger)
- Have a recent, significant loss (especially a relationship)
- Become preoccupied with death and dying
- Talk about suicide, death, or "no reason to live"
- Have attempts at suicide before
- Have observable signs of depression:
- Unrelenting low mood

- Pessimism
- Hopelessness
- Desperation
- Anxiety, psychic pain
- Withdrawal
- Sleep problems
- Increase in alcohol and other drugs
- Be faced with a humiliation or failure
- Take unnecessary risks-be reckless and impulsive
- Having a history of violence or hostility
- Making a plan
- Giving away possessions
- Obtaining means of killing oneself (e.g. rope, firearms, medication)
- Can't stop the pain, think clearly, make decisions. See any way out, sleep/eat/work (school), make the sadness go away, see the possibility of change, see themselves as worthwhile, get someone's attention, seem to get control

To have four suicides in a five month span, all from one particular high school drew a lot of attention. Cherelle wasn't in the Hill Bitches gang, but they sure did want her there. They taunted her whenever they had the chance in school, and they even beat her up out on the street. Cherelle wrote all her memories down in her diary, which sparked up the FBI investigation into the 4-block gang, when I had to prove to the police that Cherelle wasn't into gang activity.

As of today, April 2013, there have been no more suicides in Schenectady. Cherelle's life wasn't taken in vain. She brought awareness to the community and stopped the Demon!

In 2012, I wrote a poem for Cherelle's birthday and it goes like this:

"Never Again"

It's November again
And you're another year older
But your looks will never change, Cherelle,
For you will never grow older
Another birthday has come
And I sit here all alone
You're 18 now, honey
With a big black head stone

FORGOT TO SAY GOODBYE

It's been 3 years and 7 months
Since I saw your smiling face
You've put me through hell
I 'thank God for Amazing Grace
I look at your pictures all the time, Cherelle
Wondering exactly where I went wrong
How could you take away the very life I gave you?
This is no pretty love song

In 2013 my small family moved again, totaling four moves since Cherelle had passed. This time we move around the block from 213 Victory Avenue, where Cherelle took her last breath. It's nice to finally be back and look at the house again. I sometimes wish I could wander up the steps to the front window and peer in, hoping to see Cherelle sitting on the couch or something, but I know that will never happen.

Anyways, one of my old acquaintances from the neighborhood saw me at the end of March 2013 and told to me that, "No one is able to stay living at 213 Victory Ave. They don't last there long at all; the upstairs apartment stays filled, but the downstairs is always vacant." I was shocked to hear this. Maybe Cherelle haunts it. You never know!

On Cherelle's first anniversary of her death I had placed a rose at 213 Victory Avenue, went to her grave site and placed fresh flowers with her father, than had a get-together at my house with food, beverages, and conversation. I also had a small colorful book set out for people to write their memories of Cherelle in. Her father and I also had a memorial placed in the *Schenectady Gazette* newspaper, which read, "We love you and miss you with all our heart and soul."

The second anniversary I placed another flower at 213 Victory Ave and then went out to eat with her father, sister, and brother, after placing fresh flowers on her grave. Her father and I also had another memorial placed in the *Schenectady Gazette* which read "You're always in our hearts and always on our minds. We will miss you forever. Love mom, Dad, and family."

On Cherelle's third anniversary, I placed another flower at 213 Victory Ave and placed fresh flowers on her grave. I also made her favorite meal at home, which was a whole chicken, with rice, corn, cranberry sauce, and gravy. Man, could she eat some chicken.

FORGOT TO SAY GOODBYE

On Cherelle's fourth anniversary of her death, I left a long stem rose on the windowsill at 213 Victory Ave in memory of her, and then then I went to the gravesite where her body rests, but not her spirit. I left another long stem rose, and my best friend Russ left a pink balloon, on which he wrote, "I love you, Cherelle, Love Russ Forever." I had a blue balloon, but it popped on my way to the cemetery. It was really cold out, so we didn't stay more than twenty minutes long. I also made a small spread of food for Cherelle's family and friends that evening, such as Ziti, tossed salad, jello jiggles, deviled eggs, cupcakes, chocolate cookies and sugar cookies. It was nice to see everyone, but I had found six videos of Cherelle earlier in the day, and watching them threw me off the deep end.

CHAPTER 15

Memories

Throughout Cherelle's life she came across many people who have many good memories of her. The following are a few of them:

Russ has known Cherelle all her life and has known me since I was sixteen years old, so he has a lot of memories of Cherelle, some good and some not so good (she was naughty at times). He remembers when she was young, they used to watch Sesame Street together, and she would jump and dance all around and sing.

One particular time was when we all went to the Altamont Fair with Russ. He remembers taking Cherelle to the circus. Oh how she loved the clowns. She really enjoyed herself. Then came the rides: "Russ can we go on the rides," she yelled, and off she went towards the rides.

Another time Russ recalls was at Central Park. They had a big festival with rides, food, and attractions. Cherelle wanted to do them all, of course. "Russ, can I go on the swing?" "Ok," replied Russ, as he gave her money. Then came the Bouncy Bounce, then the food. "Two hot dogs, please," Russ recalls asking.

I remember every morning Cherelle woke up to "No Soggy Cereal," I would say. She hated soggy cereal. She would pop right up.

Cherelle loved the lights and attractions of the Big City, New York City, of course, but most of all, she loved the Broadway shows. I remember when she went to see *Wicked*, the musical on Broadway in New York City with her 8th grade class. It was amazing, but most of all I remember the look on my daughter's face when they opened up the curtain; it was breath-taking. She was so happy to be there. That was the first Broadway show, but not the last. We and her family came down again, another time to the Big Apple to watch *Rent*. Then we saw *Cats* at Proctors in Schenectady. Cherelle just loved musicals, of course. She loved to sing.

Cherelle and I had a fascination for paint-by-numbers. We would sit together for hours and just paint; however, I seem to always complete mine first making Cherelle angry and she would state, "You cheated Mommy!" Cherelle must have painted over 20

Paint-by-numbers in her life, and I have them all, but the one her dad has.

Cherelle was a very creative child. She used to make beautiful friendship bracelets out of plastic string and floss so quickly, even the real difficult and challenging designs.

One day Cherelle decided that her bedroom wall was a piece of paper and wrote whatever came to her mind; then what ever came to her friends' minds. They wrote down, too. So you would find things like 'Cherelle was here,' 'Tynni was here,' 'Cherelle loves Duane,' etc. However, Cherelle also wrote RIP Daddy Joe, RIP Mary, RIP Devine, which wasn't too healthy.

I remember one time when Cherelle made Collard Greens with me. It was so much fun. She did a great job, but she didn't leave much for anyone else to eat when dinner was done.

I do know for a fact that Cherelle loved her sneakers. She had several different types of stylish Nike sneakers; she never wore anything else. Cherelle even cut out pictures of sneakers and put them on her note books, books, and even her walls.

Memories of Cherelle and me gazing at all the busy people on Broadway impressed us as we sat in the Villa Italia's large store-front window. We sat there for hours eating our Italian ice cream; her favorite was strawberry. Man could that girl eat!

I also recall Cherelle riding her light blue Schwinn bike at Grandma's house. all suited up with her helmet on and all. It was funny because she'd ride a couple blocks then call us to go pick her and the bike up. No one said she was an athlete.

Cheyenne recalls Cherelle's long legs and the way she use to strut when she walked with her butt shaking back and forth. She used to walk really fast.

When I spoke to my very best friend of 24 years, named Moe, he recalled always telling his son Jordan and Cherelle when they were in 2nd grade they could not be boyfriend and girlfriend, that they were just too young to be going out with each other, but they remained friends up until Cherelle died.

Jordan's mother recalled always saying that Jordan and Cherelle were going to get married someday.

Moe also recalled Cherelle's beautiful singing voice and so do I. Cherelle would always be singing all day long, every minute she possibly could, she would. Cherelle would have made it on American Idol.

My mother has so many memories of Cherelle that it's hard for her to discuss them to this day, but she did recall a few for me for me. One in particular memory she had was when Cherelle was a little girl, she would sing a lullaby to her when she would cuddle with her and that went like this:

When I was just a little girl
I ask my mother
What will I be
Will I be pretty
Will I be rich…and this is what she said to me
K sir ra sir ra
The future is not ours to see
What will be will be
K sir ra sir ra

Another memory that her Grandmother has is that she would always rub Cherelle's temples when she was in bed falling asleep. She loved that so much that she was asleep within thirty seconds; it was so soothing to her.

My mother also recalled that whenever Cherelle would leave her house or hang up the telephone they would say to each other, "I love you whole wide world and back again and longer than forever." They never said 'Goobye' without saying those words, except one time.

When Cherelle lived with my parents, my mother said she used to do her homework upstairs on the second floor and continue talking to Grandma like she was in the room next to her. It used to drive my mother crazy because she could never hear what Cherelle was saying and she would have to yell up the stairs "What Relly? What Relly? "What Relly," all night long.

One other funny thing Cherelle did for several years was to drink or save those little creamers that you get with your coffee from a restaurant. She would then use them at home when she had her Tea Parties or just drink them like they were water or something.

One day in November 1996, when I was receiving a Christmas turkey from the county, the Gazette newspaper snapped a shot of Cherelle reaching out for the turkey and put it in the newspaper. It was really cute.

It's real hard for Darrien, Cherelle's brother, to speak on memory, but he did enlighten me with one strong memory he had of Cherelle always taking him on long walks through the hood to Duane's house or just out cruising the streets.

Debi also recalls this one experience of going out to the Glenville Queen Diner for dinner, and Cherelle ordered her food like usual, but when it came and the waitress asked, "Can I get you anything else right now?" Cherelle responded, "The garlic salt, please." That's my girl. She loved her some garlic salt.

My sister Debi has so many loving memories of Cherelle that, she too, could write a book. There was one time, she stated, that Cherelle stayed over her house and made two trays of Jell-O Jigglers for all the kids, but when they were done, no one wanted any so she said, "Ok, fine, I'll eat them all by myself." And that's just what she did.

My niece Brianna had one funny, but quite embarrassing memory. Cherelle and Brianna went to Burnt Hills Junior High School for one full year together, so they would eventually pass each other in the halls, or in Cherelle's case see her at the opposite end of the hall and yell, "Hi Bri. Bri." At the time, like any of us, she was embarrassed and just wanted to crawl in the first opened locker. You've just got to love Cherelle. She was just such a happy kid.

You know, I thought I had known Death. I had walked with it several times before with family members and friends, but Cherelle was different, she left a large void in my life that can't ever be filled.

Photos

Lisa Seymour (mother), DeVaughn Clarke (father) and Cherelle at her baptismal in 1995.

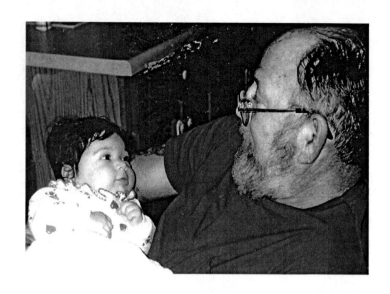

Cherelle and her Papa admiring each other
at Grandpa's house in March 1995.

Lisa Seymour (mom) and Cherelle on her first vacation in the summer of 1995 at Aunt Sherry's house in New Jersey.

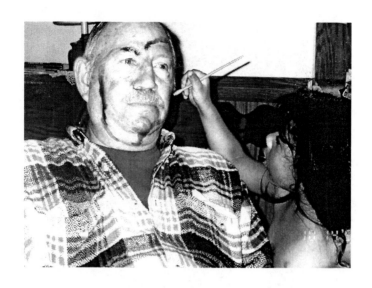

Cherelle painting Papa's face with face paint in 1998. They always had a special bond between them.

Cherelle and Lisa (mom) at 'Bring your daughter to work day', when I was working as a Therapist.

Cherelle and her younger sister Cheyenne Clarke looking cute as ever in 1999.

My three children, Cherelle, Cheyenne, and my son Darrien on Cherelle's first day of school in 2000 (first grade). She lived at 806 Bradt Street, Schenectady at that time

Cherelle's fourth grade school picture.

Cherelle's last Christmas 2008.
She just opened up a whole bunch of gum
that she had requested for Christmas.
She seemed so happy then.

Darrien Cheyenne, and Cherelle on
Thanksgiving 2008, her last Thanksgiving

Cherelle looking gorgeous, as usual. She was 13 years old.

Cherelle's spring school picture from 2007-2008 school year from Burnt Hills Ballston Lake Jr. High School.

This is the picture that made Cherelle's name known in the local newspaper. She was just 13 years old.

Suicide Awareness, Prevention, Campaigns and Support Groups

International

International Association for Suicide Prevention IASP is dedicated to preventing suicidal behaviour, to alleviate its effects, and to provide a forum for academians, mental health professionals, crisis workers, volunteers and suicide survivors.

United Kingdom

Choose Life: A National Strategy and Action Plan to Prevent Suicide in Scotland

Centre For Suicide Research - The Centre is based in the University of Oxford Department of Psychiatry. Professor Keith Hawton is its Director. The work of the research group is focused on investigation of the causes, treatment and prevention of suicidal behaviour.

Scottish Association for Mental Health - After A Suicide - SAMH has written a booklet for people bereaved as a result of suicide in Scotland. As well as providing practical information about issues like funeral expenses, registering the death etc, this booklet also suggests coping strategies for people to try, and includes details of agencies which might be able to help.

University of Oxford - Centre for Suicide Research The Centre is based in the University of Oxford Department of Psychiatry. Professor Keith Hawton is its Director. Professor Mark Williams also leads a research group within the Centre. The overall research programme of the Centre is focused on investigation of the causes, treatment and prevention of suicidal behaviour.

Ireland

The Irish Association of Suicidology - The Irish Association of Suicidology had its inaugural meeting in 1996. Since then it has had seven annual meetings each dealing with various aspects of suicide and suicidal behaviour in a general way. They recognise the complexity of the issues involved in suicide prevention. Simplistic responses are to be avoided.

United States

American Foundation for Suicide Prevention (AFSP) - The American Foundation for Suicide Prevention, a 501(c)(3) organisation, has been at the forefront of a wide range of suicide prevention initiatives in 2009 -- each designed to reduce loss of life from suicide. They are investing in groundbreaking research, new educational campaigns, innovative demonstration projects and critical policy work. They are are expanding their assistance to people whose lives have been affected by suicide, reaching out to offer support and offering opportunities to become involved in prevention.

Fierce Goodbye Fierce Goodbye will be airing on Hallmark Channel on Sunday, August 22 at noon (ET/PT). family survivors of suicide share personal stories of their trauma. Mental health experts talk about the stigma of mental illness and suicide, and theologians and biblical scholars spell out traditional views on what happens to the "soul" after suicide and how some views are changing in light of new knowledge about mental illness. A copy of the documentary video may be ordered through the site.

National Strategy For Suicide Prevention

Prevent Suicide - Information to help educate the public on Suicide

Prevent Suicide Now

Save: Suicide Awareness Voices of Education - The SAVE mission is to prevent suicide through public awareness and education, reduce stigma, and serve as a resource for those touched by suicide.

Suicide.org - Suicide.org conducts extensive work online and offline to further its mission of suicide prevention, awareness, and support. In addition to operating Suicide.org, which is the largest and most-visited suicide-related site in the world, we own and operate numerous additional critical sites, including HurricaneKatrina.com, Tsunamis.com, America911.com, OklahomaCityBombing.com, VirginiaTechMassacre.com, RapeHelp.com, VietnamMemorial.com, MilitaryHeroes.com, EatingDisorderHelp.com, SelfInjuryHelp.com, GriefAndLoss.com, and numerous others. We assist countless individuals via these websites. And we constantly develop new sites.

Suicide Prevention Action Network USA

Suicide Prevention Resource Center (SPRC)

The Fred Fund The Fred Fund provides basic resources and links to information for families and children who have experienced the loss of loved ones to suicide, or those who may be experiencing depression. Survivors of suicide are also encouraged to submit memorial stories as a means of healing, empowerment and sharing.

Yellow Ribbon Suicide Prevention Program

Canada

Suicide Information & Education Centre - The Suicide Information & Education Centre (SIEC) is a special library and resource centre providing information on suicide and suicidal behaviour.

Australia

Australian Institute of Family Studies - Developed by the Australian Institute of Family Studies, this resource is to help those working to prevent suicide.

Youth Suicide and Self-Injury In Australia - This supplement presents some descriptive data on youth suicide in Australia. It is largely based on Australian deaths data up to 1995, though some sections are also based on Australian hospital morbidity data and on international mortality data.

Depression & Overdose Prevention in Youths and Teens - Suicide Prevention information service with suicide and depression information, statistics and help Australia wide.

Relationship Counseling & Christian Guidance - Humaneed: marriage, relationship and family counseling and guidance service based in Melbourne, Victoria. We improve relationships by resolving marriage issues like communication and intimacy or affairs.

New Zealand

Ministry of Health - Suicide Prevention in New Zealand

Europe

European Network for Suicidology National and International Organisations and Associations in Research and Suicide-Prevention.

Suicide is NEVER the answer,
getting help is the answer.
If you are suicidal, have attempted suicide,
or are a suicide survivor,
you will find help, hope, comfort, understanding,
support, love, and extensive resources here.

www.suicide.org

CPSIA information can be obtained at www.ICGtesting.com
Printed in the USA
BVOW05s0123110314

347280BV00007B/40/P